50 Sex Tokens For Your Pleasure :)

This Belongs To:

_____

Give me the best blow job you've ever given!

Give me a lap dance in your own unique style...no one else turns me on like you do!

Good for a full body massage with a happy ending :)

Let me blindfold you and:

_____

_____

Undress slowly for me and let me
masturbate just looking at you...
you're so fucking hot!

New
position
we've never
tried before

Let me either:

- shave your pussy and eat it
- paint your nails my color of choice and then you give me a hand job
- paint your toe nails my color of choice and then you give me a foot job

*Circle as desired

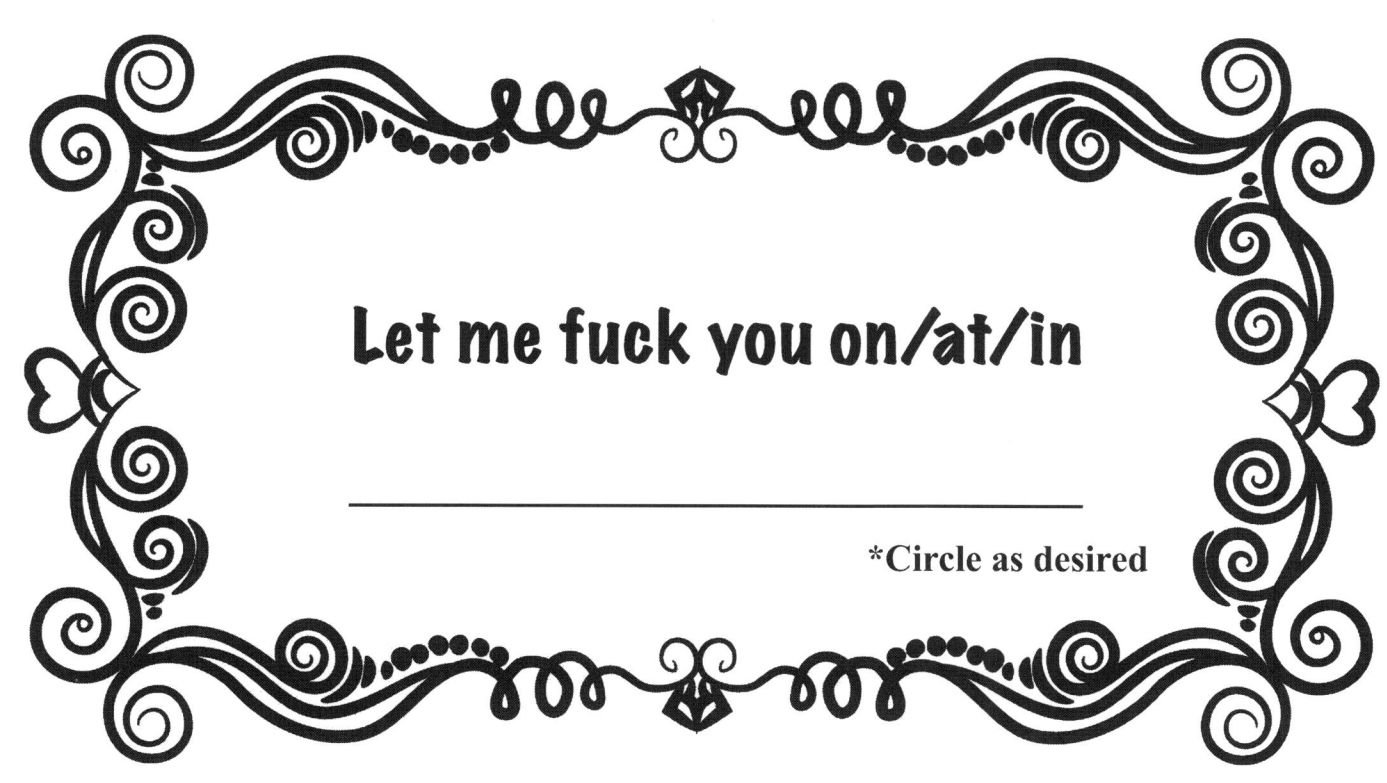

Let me fuck you on/at/in

_____

*Circle as desired

Role Play

Me:

You:

Good for one erotic movie of my choice.

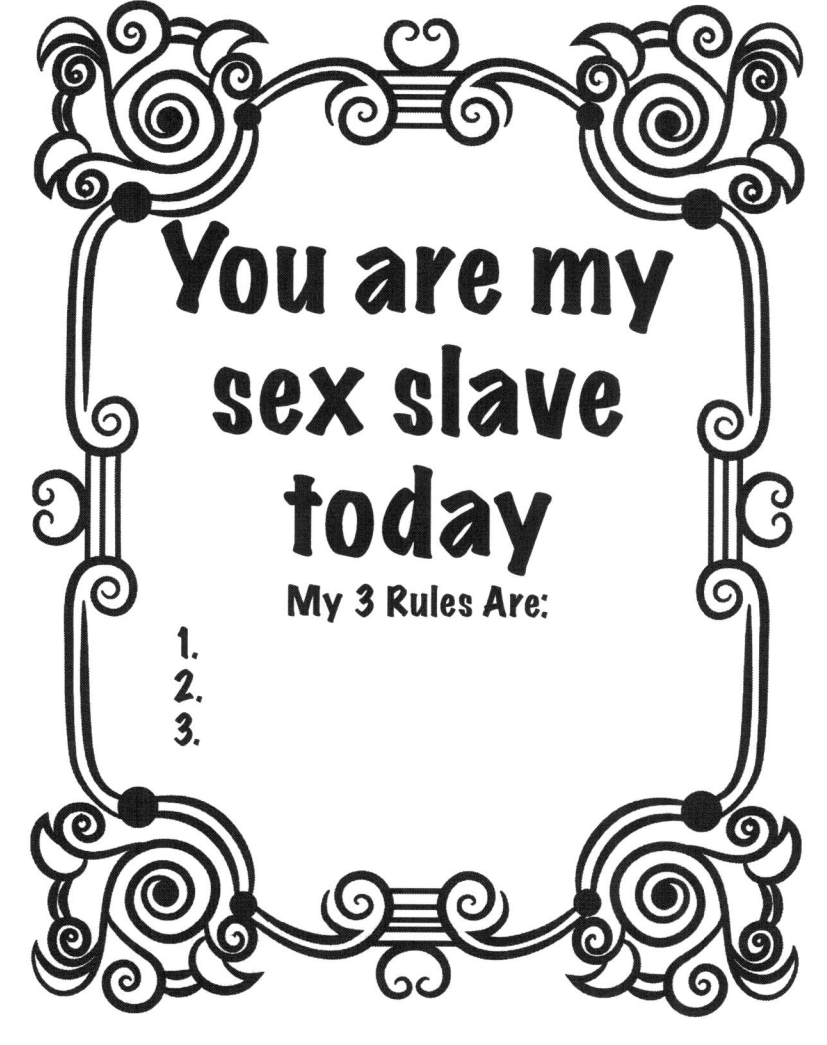

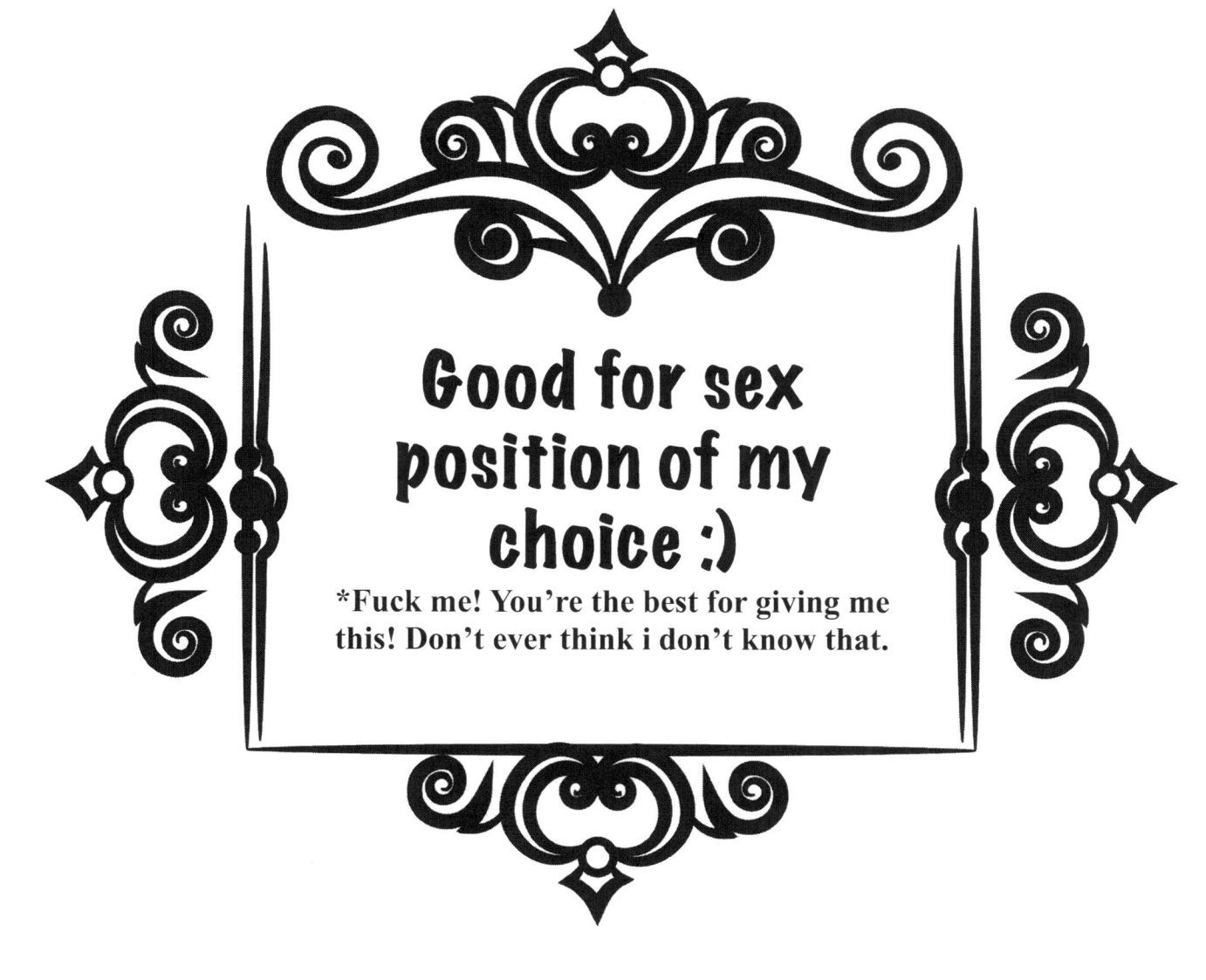

Good for sex position of my choice :)

*Fuck me! You're the best for giving me this! Don't ever think i don't know that.

Outdoor Sex

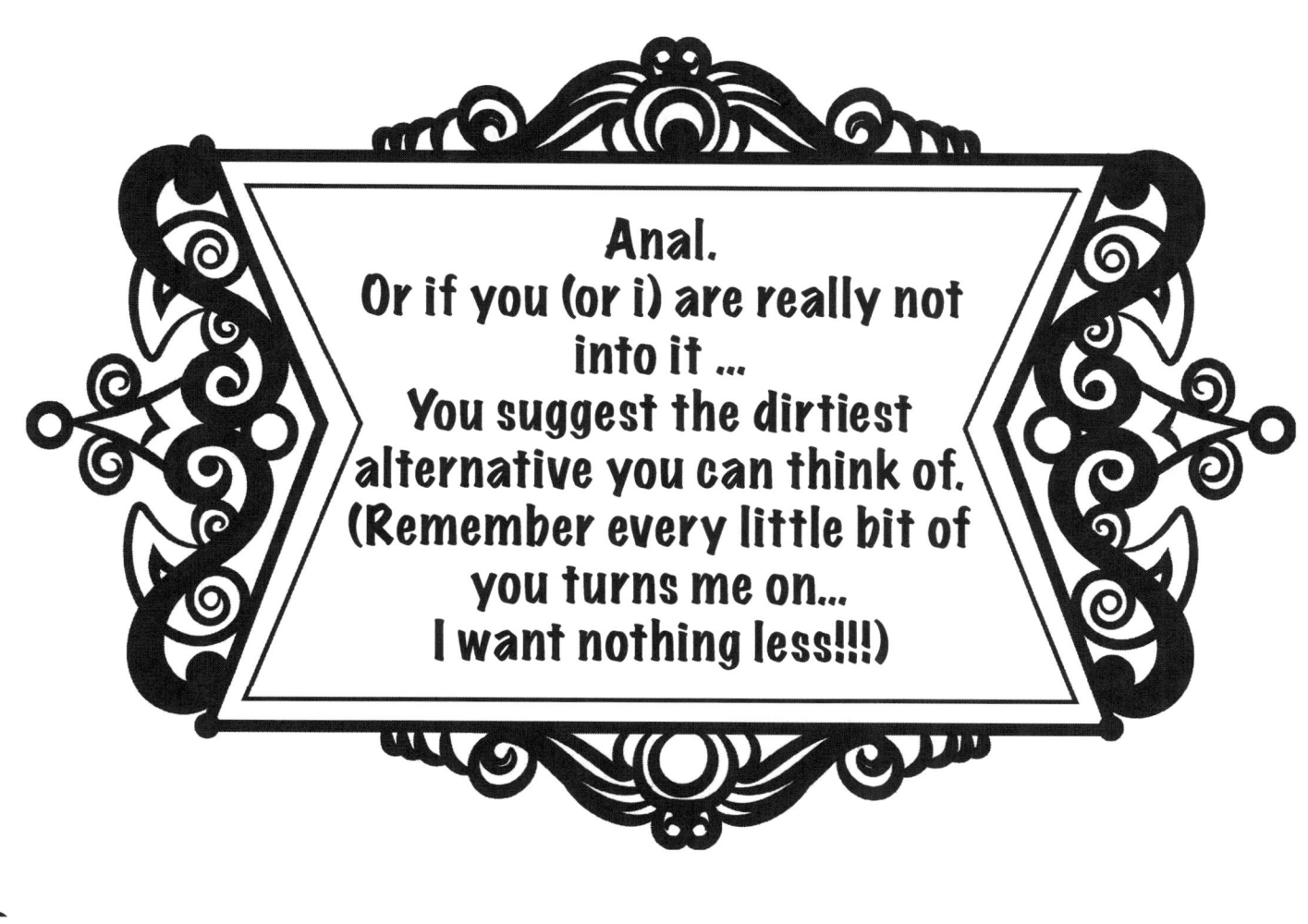

Anal.
Or if you (or i) are really not into it ...
You suggest the dirtiest alternative you can think of.
(Remember every little bit of you turns me on...
I want nothing less!!!)

Ride me in a way to drive me crazy till i cum.

Spank me ☐
I want to spank you ☐

*tick as desired

*Circle depending on your mood

Let's fuck/make love
as we watch...

Cook me dinner naked
OR
Get naked, lay down on the kitchen table and put my fave desert all over you and let me eat it off slowly piece by piece...
You get to decide! See how considerate i am! :)

No matter where we are or when, (i'll always look out for you and protect you)... let me fuck you when i give you this.

Send me a really dirty text today...

Wear _____
for me and let's fuck
till i can't cum
anymore...

Tell me your
fantasy...
be honest!
I want to fulfil it :)

Wake me up
with a
blowjob :)

I want you to:

_____

_____

_____

_____

BDSM Sex Session

Let's explore our boundaries together....

Let me _____
for however long i want,
listening to a soundtrack of
my choice.

Good for make up
sex after we've
had an argument

Do that one
thing you know i
like but you
never want to do

I want you to:

_____

_____

Fuck me
in the

_____

Talk dirty to me for 20 minutes as we make out real slow...

Wear _____

for me and let's

_____

_____

Strip
Poker

I want you to:

_____

_____

Dress up for me wearing

and let's go out to

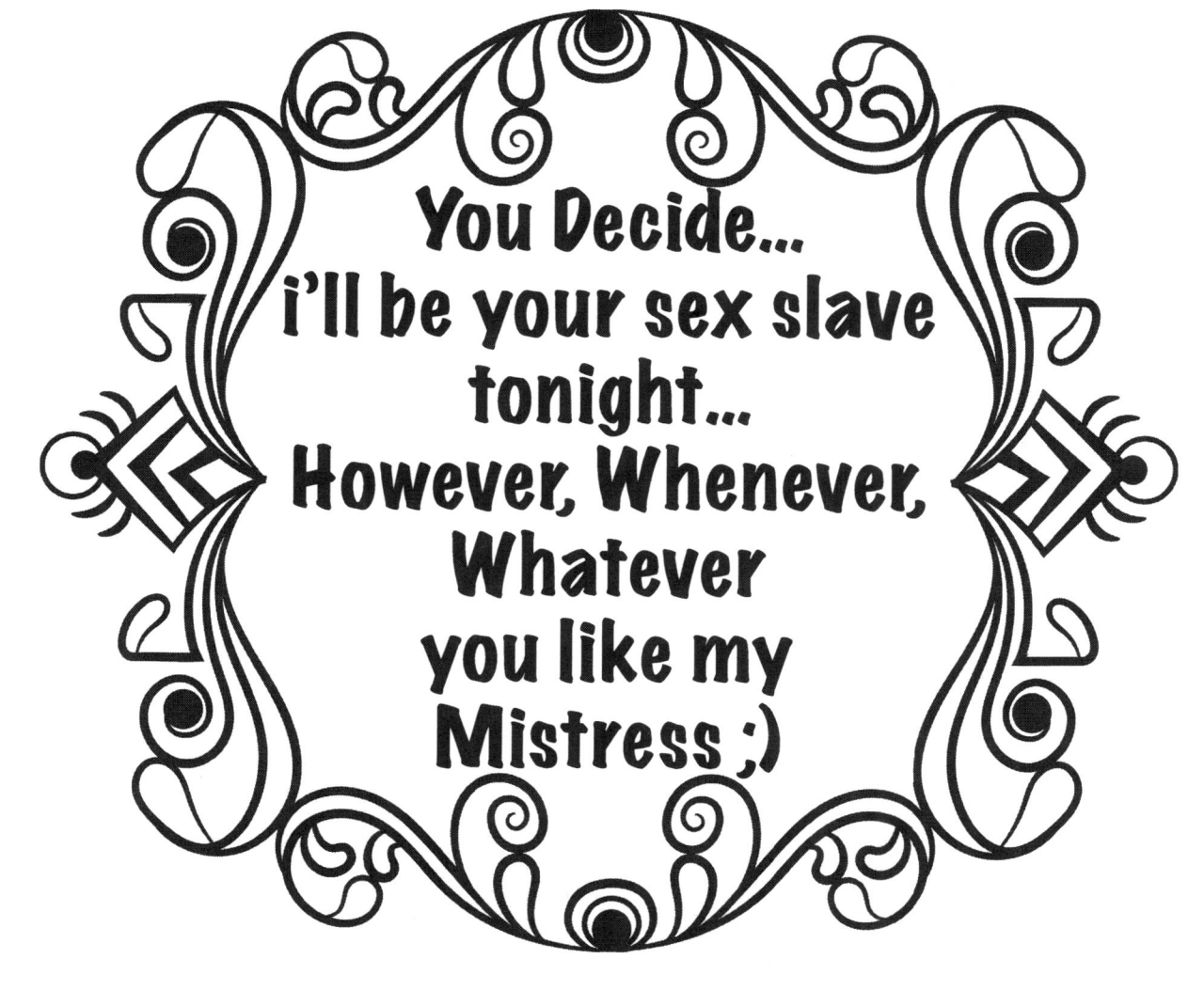

You're so fucking hot!
Let me watch you masturbate with
a vibrator till you cum

Sex Weekend Vacation or Staycation

* You & Me...Food, Drink and Sex All Weekend!

Made in the USA
Middletown, DE
13 November 2019